Summer 2005

East
    Texas
        Oil
Museum

BLUEBONNET

at the East Texas Oil Museum

BLUEBONNET

at the East Texas Oil Museum

By Mary Brooke Casad
Illustrated by Benjamin Vincent

PELICAN PUBLISHING COMPANY
Gretna 2005

For my nieces and nephews—Christopher, Matthew,
Andrew, Mitchell, Erin, Katy, Grant, Ben, Alex, Irene,
and Lillian—with love from "Aunt Brookie"

The author gratefully acknowledges Joe White, director of the
East Texas Oil Museum; Claud Wallace; and Guy and Billie
Oliphint for their contributions to the story.

Library of Congress Cataloging-in-Publication Data

Casad, Mary Brooke.
    Bluebonnet at the East Texas Oil Museum / by Mary Brooke
Casad ; illustrated by Benjamin Vincent.
       p. cm.
    Summary: Bluebonnet the Armadillo visits her sister and
her family, and they go to a museum dedicated to the oil fields
of East Texas.
    ISBN-13: 978-1-58980-358-9 (hardcover : alk. paper)
  [1. Oil fields—Fiction. 2. Texas—Fiction. 3. Armadillos—
Fiction.] I. Vincent, Benjamin, ill. II. Title.
    PZ7.C265Bmm 2005
    [E]—dc22
                                 2005011286

Printed in Singapore
Published by Pelican Publishing Company, Inc.
1000 Burmaster Street, Gretna, Louisiana 70053

BLUEBONNET
AT THE EAST TEXAS OIL MUSEUM

Bluebonnet the traveling Texas armadillo ambled through the pine-tree forests of East Texas. "Surely I'm getting close to Irmadillo's burrow," she said.

It had been many years since Bluebonnet and her three sisters, Normadillo, Irmadillo, and Arvilladillo, were little armadillos, growing up in the Texas Hill Country. Armadillo "pups" are born four at a time and are either all boys or all girls.

"Hey, Bluebonnet, over here!"

Bluebonnet turned to see her sister Irmadillo, poking her head out of the ground. Bluebonnet was so excited that she ran and tumbled into the burrow. Irmadillo began to laugh.

"That was quite an entrance!" Irmadillo said, hugging her sister hello. Bluebonnet looked up into the faces of five other armadillos.

"Howdy, Bluebonnet. I'm Irmadillo's husband, 'Dad' Joiner Dillo," said the largest armadillo. "And these are our four sons: Bradford, Lloyd, Hunt, and Wildcatter."

"Hello, Aunt Bluebonnet," the four armadillo brothers said in a loud chorus.

"My, my," marveled Bluebonnet. "What a fine family you have, Irmadillo. And such interesting names."

"Their names can tell you a little bit about East Texas history," replied Irmadillo.

"I'm named for Columbus Marion 'Dad' Joiner," said "Dad" Joiner Dillo. "In 1926, 'Dad' Joiner was in Galveston. One night beneath a full moon, he walked along the beach. He soon became tired and lay down to sleep. That night he dreamed he discovered a big oil field in East Texas."

"Soon, he traveled to East Texas and found the place he had seen in his dream. It was on a farm owned by Daisy Bradford," said Bradford. "That's who I'm named for."

"Then he called his friend, Dr. A. D. Lloyd, a geologist, to help him. That's where I got my name," said Lloyd. "On October 3, 1930, the oil began to spew up from the ground. Several thousand people were there to see it. The East Texas oil boom was born!"

"Soon, 'Dad' Joiner sold several of his oil leases to H. L. Hunt, who started his own oil company," said Hunt. "I guess you figured out that's where my name came from."

"Yes," said Bluebonnet. "But what about the name Wildcatter?"

"Wildcatter is the name given to people who drill oil wells," replied Wildcatter. "The name comes from the first oil well drilled in America. That happened in Titusville, Pennsylvania in 1859, on Wild Cat Creek."

"But the East Texas oil field is one of the largest in the world," said Irmadillo. "It's produced six billion barrels of oil, and some of the wells are still pumping."

"How did you learn so much about it?" asked Bluebonnet.

"There's a museum in the town of Kilgore," said Bradford.

"On the campus of Kilgore College, home of the world-famous Kilgore Rangerettes," added Lloyd.

"The museum was given in 1980 by the Hunt family," Hunt said proudly.

"And we'd like to take you to see it, Aunt Bluebonnet," said Wildcatter. "The East Texas Oil Museum."

Bluebonnet smiled at her nephews. "Well, let's go!" she said.

"Y'all go on and have a good time," said "Dad" Joiner Dillo. "I've got to get back to work. I'm trying to dig my own oil well."

"And I'll catch up with you in a little while," said Irmadillo.

Soon, the four little armadillos and Bluebonnet approached a building with a large wooden tower by the front door. "Here we are, Aunt Bluebonnet!" the four brothers squealed. "The original oil derricks were made of wood, just like that one."

Bradford opened the door of the museum. Bluebonnet and her nephews scurried in.

"This way, Aunt Bluebonnet." Lloyd motioned for her to follow him.

"Look up," said Hunt, pointing to a large wall mural.

"When the East Texas oil field was discovered, it was the largest oil field in the world," said Wildcatter. "Thirty-two thousand wells were drilled over forty-two miles."

"Life in East Texas was very different back then," said Bradford. He held a receiver to Bluebonnet's ear. "Just listen to this."

Bluebonnet listened to the voices of long ago describe the homes, churches, schools, and towns of the 1930s. Then she closed her eyes.

"What are you doing, Aunt Bluebonnet?" Lloyd asked.

"I'm trying to imagine what East Texas must have looked like in the 1930s when oil was discovered," she answered.

The four brothers giggled. "All you have to do is walk through those doors!"

Bluebonnet's eyes grew wide as her nephews guided her through a door.

"Welcome to Boomtown, U.S.A.!" they shouted.

Bluebonnet blinked. She was standing on the board
sidewalk of an old-timey town!

"It's like we've stepped back in time," gasped
Bluebonnet.
Honk, honk! Beep, beep!

"Watch out, Aunt Bluebonnet!" hollered Hunt as a car drove by, splattering mud on the sidewalk.

"Hey, let's have an ice-cream sundae at the Overton Drug Store," said Wildcatter. Soon the armadillos were seated at the soda counter, enjoying their treats.

"Look, Dr. Lloyd and 'Dad' Joiner are having their picture taken," said Bradford, pointing to the photography studio.

Lloyd jumped down from his stool and posed alongside Dr. Lloyd just as the camera flashed.

"Lloyd, what are you doing?" cried Bluebonnet.

"I just wanted to have my picture taken with the man I was named for," said Lloyd with a big grin. The armadillos finished their ice cream and headed across the muddy street.

"What's at the Gladewater Museum?" asked Bluebonnet, reading a sign.

"An elevator ride to the center of the earth!" said Hunt. "Climb aboard!"

As the armadillos took their seats in the large elevator, the doors closed and the lights went out. *Bang! Thud!* The elevator began to move with a jolt.

"What's happening?" Bluebonnet whispered loudly.

"We're going down deep into the earth, just like the oil drills," said Wildcatter.

"Howdy, folks! I'm Hank, and this is Professor Rockbottom. We'll be your guides on this journey to the center of the earth." The armadillos listened as the guides explained the layers of rock beneath the surface of the earth. Each time the elevator stopped, doors opened behind a glass window to reveal the different rock layers.

"So Texas was once covered by the ocean," Bluebonnet said.

"And the fossils of sea life created oil," said Bradford.

The elevator continued its descent. "We're almost to the Woodbine sandstone layer, Aunt Bluebonnet," said Lloyd.

"That's 3,650 feet below the earth's surface, where the oil is!" shouted Wildcatter. "And look, here comes a drill!"

"Looks like someone is drilling for oil!" said Hank and Professor Rockbottom. "We'd better head back up!" The elevator quickly rose until the doors opened and the armadillos stepped off.

"That's the deepest burrow I've ever been in!" said Bluebonnet.

"I think we should go to the picture show now,"
suggested Bradford.
"What's the movie?" asked Bluebonnet.

"The Great East Texas Oil Boom," said Hunt, pointing to the movie marquee. "And don't forget the popcorn!"

Bluebonnet and her nephews took their seats in the theater. Soon the lights dimmed and the curtains opened. "Shh! The movie is starting," Bluebonnet said, munching popcorn. The black-and-white film flickered across the screen.

"Look at that muddy street," said Lloyd. "There was lots of rain when the oil boom began."

"So many people came to East Texas when oil was discovered," said Wildcatter. "Everyone was hoping to become a 'wildcatter' and dig an oil well."

"Wow! There were 1,100 oil wells in Kilgore," said Bradford. "'The World's Richest Acre' in downtown Kilgore had twenty-four wells."

"The 'Big Inch' pipeline ran all the way from the East Texas oil field to New Jersey and provided America with the oil they needed in World War II," said Hunt.

"Look, boys, it's the Daisy Bradford #3, the oil well that started the boom," said Bluebonnet, pointing to the screen. The armadillos watched as the movie captured the oil gusher on film, shooting high into the air. Suddenly, the theater seats began to shake. "Do you feel something moving?" Bluebonnet asked.

"The ground is trembling, just like it did when the oil blew out of the ground," said Lloyd.

"Boys! Bluebonnet!" Irmadillo rushed into the theater, out of breath. "Come quick and see! 'Dad' Joiner Dillo has hit a gusher!"

Bluebonnet and her nephews followed Irmadillo through the piney woods. Soon they reached an oil derrick, where oil was spewing out from the ground. "Dad" Joiner Dillo was smiling proudly.

"I did it!" he shouted. "All my hard work of digging finally paid off!"

"Hooray!" cheered Irmadillo, Bradford, Lloyd, Hunt, and Wildcatter.

"Perhaps next time I visit, your picture will be in the East Texas Oil Museum," said Bluebonnet. And she waved good-bye as she headed off for more Texas travels.